Green Constellations

Intersection of Hemp and Zodiac

MATTHEW PETCHINSKY

Apophis Enterprises LLC

GREEN CONSTELLATIONS

Chapter 1

Green Constellations: Intersection of Hemp and Zodiac
By: Matthew Petchinsky

Introduction 1A

Astrology has been a fascination for thousands of years, there are many different versions of it and it has had the hearts and mind of man in every culture on Earth, since mankind was primitive Caveman in a cave to Egyptian to modern man. Astrology is engrained in our DNA. Please enjoy this book.

Introduction 2B: The Celestial Tapestry of Hemp

In the grand, interwoven fabric of human history and the cosmos, few threads are as uniquely intertwined as those of hemp (Cannabis sativa) and astrology. This exploration delves into the ancient and mystical connections between the cosmos and cannabis, revealing how the plant has been perceived, utilized, and revered across various cultures and epochs. Our journey traverses the sacred relationship between hemp and astrological beliefs, highlighting its significant influence on human civilization.

Hemp, a plant that has clothed, healed, and nourished humanity for thousands of years, also holds a place in the spiritual and mystical practices of many cultures. Its deep roots in human history are matched by an equally profound connection to the celestial, where it has been seen as a symbol of enlightenment, healing, and even a bridge to the divine. This exploration seeks to understand how the stars and the cycles of the zodiac have intertwined with the cultivation, use, and cultural significance of hemp.

From ancient astrologers who observed the heavens for signs to guide their agricultural practices, including the planting and harvesting of hemp, to modern interpretations of hemp's role in aligning with cosmic energies, this narrative uncovers the multifaceted layers of this relationship. We delve into ancient texts and astrological alignments to uncover how hemp has been aligned with specific zodiac signs, influencing its cultivation and ceremonial use. Through this lens, we aim to provide a richer understanding of hemp's place in the tapestry of human belief and its sacred connection to the stars.

The journey through the green constellations illuminates how hemp's versatile nature – from its use in textiles, medicine, and nutrition to its role in rituals and ceremonies – mirrors the complex and dynamic patterns of the cosmos. As we explore the intersection of hemp and the zodiac, we uncover stories of harmony between earthly and celestial realms, revealing insights into how ancient cultures sought to understand and influence their world through the sacred plant and the stars.

This exploration is not merely historical; it also reflects on contemporary understandings and reimaginings of these ancient connections. In an age where sustainability and harmony with nature are increasingly at the forefront of global consciousness, revisiting the sacred bonds between hemp and astrology offers insights into pathways for aligning modern life with the rhythms of the cosmos. By understanding how our ancestors viewed and utilized these connections, we can inspire a renewed sense of interconnectedness with the universe, grounded in the enduring legacy of hemp.

Thus, the celestial tapestry of hemp invites us to weave together past knowledge and present aspirations, guiding us toward a future where the ancient wisdom of the stars and the earth's bounty are once again revered and integrated into the fabric of human life. Through this journey, we rediscover the profound connections that bind us to the cosmos, with hemp serving as a symbol of unity, healing, and cosmic harmony.

CHAPTER 1: COSMIC ORIGINS OF CANNABIS

The story of cannabis, or hemp as it is also known, is as old as civilization itself, with its origins entwined in the fabric of the cosmos. This chapter embarks on a journey to unearth the ancient civilizations' reverence for cannabis and its celestial associations, weaving through stories and myths from around the world that illustrate hemp's esteemed position in spiritual and daily life, intertwined with the stars.

Ancient Civilizations and Celestial Reverence

The cultivation of cannabis dates back over 10,000 years, making it one of humanity's oldest crops. Ancient civilizations not only recognized cannabis for its practical uses in textiles, medicine, and food but also revered it for its spiritual significance. These societies observed the heavens with keen interest, believing the movements of celestial bodies influenced terrestrial life. Within this cosmic dance, cannabis held a special place, often associated with deities, fertility, and cosmic harmony.

In ancient China, hemp was considered a gift from the divine, integral to rituals and medicine. The Chinese goddess Magu, often depicted with hemp, symbolized healing and longevity, embodying the sacred bond between humans, hemp, and the heavens. The Shennong Bencaojing, an ancient Chinese pharmacopeia, lists cannabis as a superior herb, highlighting its importance in aligning the physical and spiritual realms.

Similarly, the ancient Vedic texts of India revered cannabis as one of five sacred plants. The Rigveda, composed over 3,000 years ago, sings praises of a celestial plant, bhang (cannabis), associating it with the god Shiva. Legend has it that Shiva wandered into the fields after a family dispute and found solace under a cannabis plant. This divine encounter led to cannabis being cherished as a gift from the gods, capable of alleviating anxiety and bringing spiritual insight.

Cannabis in Myth and Astrology

The relationship between cannabis and the cosmos is also reflected in the myths and astrology of ancient civilizations. Astrologers, priests, and shamans looked to the stars for guidance on when to plant and harvest cannabis, believing that its growth was influenced by the constellations. In Babylon and Assyria, hemp was associated with the planet Venus, symbolizing love, fertility, and beauty — echoing the plant's life-giving properties.

In ancient Egypt, cannabis was used in ceremonies to honor the goddess Seshat, the deity of wisdom, knowledge, and writing. Seshat was often depicted with a seven-pointed leaf above her head, reminiscent of a cannabis leaf, suggesting a celestial link between the plant and divine knowledge. This sacred relationship underscored the belief that cannabis could open the mind to higher consciousness and cosmic truths.

The Scythians, a nomadic tribe known for their mastery of horseback riding and fierce warrior culture, used cannabis in funeral rituals to cleanse the body and spirit, facilitating the journey of the deceased into the afterlife. Herodotus, the Greek historian, wrote of the Scythians throwing hemp seeds onto hot stones to create a vapor that induced a state of divine ecstasy, connecting them with the spirit world.

The Zodiac and Cannabis

The zodiac, a celestial circle of twelve 30° divisions of celestial longitude that are centered upon the ecliptic, has played a significant role in agricultural practices and spiritual beliefs. Each zodiac sign has been historically associated with certain plants, and cannabis, with its versatile and enduring nature, has been linked to several signs, reflecting its multifaceted significance.

Pisces, known for its deep spiritual and emotional realms, resonates with cannabis's ability to induce introspection and enlightenment. Virgo's association with health and healing mirrors cannabis's medicinal properties. Sagittarius, symbolizing the quest for knowledge and truth, parallels the plant's role in expanding consciousness and understanding.

Conclusion

The cosmic origins of cannabis reveal a profound connection between ancient civilizations, their celestial beliefs, and this versatile plant. Through stories and myths from around the globe, we see how cannabis has been revered as a sacred link between the earthly and the divine, influenced by the stars and embedded in the spiritual fabric of societies. As we continue to explore the intersection of hemp and the zodiac, we uncover not only the historical significance of cannabis but also its enduring legacy as a plant of cosmic harmony and spiritual enlightenment.

If you want to see some amazing products, please visit my Virtual Dispensary: https://shift.store/sg1fan23477/retail

CHAPTER 2: HEMP THROUGH THE ASTROLOGICAL AGES

As we traverse the vast expanse of time, the relationship between hemp and the cosmos reveals itself to be ever-evolving, deeply influenced by the shifting astrological ages. Each age, corresponding to the precession of the equinoxes through the signs of the zodiac, marks a distinct epoch in human consciousness, culture, and, as we shall see, the cultivation and significance of hemp. From the fiery initiative of Aries to the intellectual enlightenment of Aquarius, this chapter outlines the journey of hemp through the astrological ages, unveiling its profound connection to the celestial movements and human evolution.

The Age of Aries (c. 2000 BCE - 0 CE)

The Age of Aries, symbolized by the Ram, heralded an era of exploration, war, and conquest. It was a time when the leadership of pharaohs, kings, and warriors was paramount. Hemp played a crucial role in this age, primarily in the form of textiles for sails, ropes, and military equipment. The versatility and durability of hemp made it indispensable for the expansion and maintenance of empires. Cultivation spread through ancient civilizations, from China to Egypt, where it supported not only the military but also the burgeoning trade routes that connected the ancient world.

The Age of Pisces (c. 1 CE - 2000 CE)

With the dawn of the Age of Pisces, symbolized by the Fish, a significant shift occurred towards spirituality, religion, and the unseen realms. This age saw the rise of major world religions, including Christianity and Islam, which deeply influenced the cultural and spiritual landscape. Hemp's role transitioned from the martial to the mystical and medicinal. In medieval Europe, hemp became a staple in everyday life, used in clothing, paper, and food. Its medicinal properties were documented by herbalists and healers, making it a common remedy in folk medicine. In the East, hemp continued to hold spiritual significance, woven into the rituals and practices of Buddhism and Hinduism.

The Transition to the Age of Aquarius (c. 2000 CE - Present)

The current Age of Aquarius, symbolized by the Water-Bearer, represents a time of knowledge, innovation, and a heightened collective consciousness. This era is marked by a resurgence in the appreciation of hemp, not just as a material resource but as a symbol of sustainability, wellness, and spiritual awakening. The cultivation and usage of hemp have seen a renaissance, driven by the environmental movement, advances in technology, and a shift towards holistic health.

Insights into the Astrological Influences

- Aries to Pisces: The transition from Aries to Pisces marked a shift from the external conquest to internal exploration. Hemp's role evolved accordingly, from supporting the physical expansion of empires to nourishing the spiritual and healing practices that flourished in Pisces. The plant's adaptability made it a constant through these shifting times, reflecting humanity's changing priorities and values.
- Pisces to Aquarius: As we moved from the Age of Pisces to the Age of Aquarius, hemp's significance has been

reinvigorated in a context of environmental consciousness and a return to natural, sustainable practices. The innovative spirit of Aquarius has led to the development of new hemp-based products, from biofuels and plastics to health foods and therapeutic uses, showcasing the plant's versatility and its alignment with contemporary values of sustainability and wellness.

· **Cultural Significance**: Each astrological age has seen hemp woven into the cultural fabric in unique ways. In Aries, it was a tool of emperors and warriors; in Pisces, a component of spiritual and medicinal practices; and in Aquarius, it symbolizes a return to harmony with nature and a forward-looking vision for humanity.

· **Cultivation and Usage**: The cultivation practices of hemp have evolved with human understanding and technological advancement. From hand-harvested crops to sophisticated cultivation techniques aimed at maximizing yield and sustainability, the way we grow hemp reflects the changing ethos of each astrological age.

Conclusion

The journey of hemp through the astrological ages offers a fascinating lens through which to view the evolution of human culture, consciousness, and technology. As we move deeper into the Age of Aquarius, hemp stands at the forefront of a paradigm shift towards sustainability, health, and global awareness. Its deep roots in the past provide a foundation for its role in our future, embodying the interconnectedness of the cosmos, Earth, and humanity. Through the ages, hemp has mirrored the celestial influences on human evolution, serving as a constant reminder of our cosmic origins and our ongoing journey through the stars.

If you want to see some amazing products, please visit my Virtual Dispensary: https://shift.store/sg1fan23477/retail

CHAPTER 3: THE ZODIAC AND THE PLANT: A MAGICAL BOND

The cosmic tapestry weaves together the zodiac and cannabis, revealing a magical bond that transcends mere physicality. This chapter delves into the unique connection each zodiac sign holds with cannabis, shaped by elemental energies (Fire, Earth, Air, Water) and planetary rulerships. We explore how these celestial influences imbue cannabis with specific vibrations that can enhance its medicinal and spiritual use, offering a deeper understanding of the plant's multifaceted nature.

Elemental Energies and Planetary Rulerships

Each zodiac sign is associated with one of the four elements — Fire, Earth, Air, Water — which represent different types of energy and modes of perception. Planetary rulerships further define these energies, endowing each sign with distinct characteristics and inclinations. Cannabis, with its versatile nature, resonates differently with the energies of each sign, offering tailored benefits and experiences.

- Fire Signs (Aries, Leo, Sagittarius): Fire represents action, inspiration, and enthusiasm. Cannabis strains that invigorate the spirit and stimulate creativity are particularly resonant with Fire signs. These individuals might find sativa strains uplifting, enhancing their natural zeal and fostering a sense of joy and adventure.
- Earth Signs (Taurus, Virgo, Capricorn): Earth signifies stability, practicality, and grounding. Indica strains, known for their relaxing and grounding effects, align well with Earth signs, offering comfort, physical ease, and help in nurturing their inner sense of peace and contentment.
- Air Signs (Gemini, Libra, Aquarius): Air denotes intellect, communication, and socialization. Hybrid strains can offer a balanced effect that stimulates the mind while keeping the body relaxed, suiting the dynamic energy of Air signs. These strains can aid in social interactions, enhance communication, and inspire innovative thinking.
- Water Signs (Cancer, Scorpio, Pisces): Water symbolizes emotion, intuition, and sensitivity. Strains with calming and soothing effects can help Water signs navigate their deep emotional seas, offering a sense of emotional stability and enhanced intuition.

Enhancing Medicinal and Spiritual Use

Understanding the bond between the zodiac signs and cannabis can significantly enhance both its medicinal and spiritual uses. By aligning cannabis use with one's zodiac sign and elemental energy, individuals can tailor their experience to match their physical, emotional, and spiritual needs.

- **Medicinal Use:** Zodiacal and elemental insights can guide the selection of cannabis strains for specific health issues. For example, an Earth sign seeking relief from stress might prefer a strain that offers relaxation without sedation, aligning with their need for stability and grounding. Similarly, a Fire sign with chronic pain may benefit from a strain that provides pain relief while also invigorating their natural energy.

- **Spiritual Use:** On a spiritual level, cannabis can be used as a tool for introspection and cosmic connection. Water signs, for instance, might use cannabis to deepen their emotional and intuitive insights during meditation, while Air signs could use it to enhance mental clarity and open new avenues of thought. By considering the elemental and zodiacal correspondences, users can select strains that amplify their spiritual journey, fostering a deeper connection to the universe.

Conclusion

The magical bond between the zodiac and cannabis is a testament to the plant's celestial heritage and its profound connection to human consciousness. By understanding and respecting this bond, individuals can unlock the full potential of cannabis, enhancing both its healing powers and its capacity to connect us with the deeper, more mystical aspects of our existence. As we navigate this green constellation, we are reminded of the intricate interplay between the cosmos, the Earth, and all living beings, with cannabis serving as a sacred bridge that unites us with the universe's vast, magical expanse.

If you want to see some amazing products, please visit my Virtual Dispensary: https://shift.store/sg1fan23477/retail

CHAPTER 4: ARIES - THE FIERY TRAILBLAZER

Aries, the first sign of the zodiac, is symbolized by the Ram and ruled by Mars, the planet of energy, action, and desire. Aries individuals are known for their fiery, pioneering spirit. They are natural leaders, brimming with courage, enthusiasm, and a zest for life. This chapter delves into the characteristics of Aries, exploring how hemp can energize and support their trailblazing nature. We will also recommend cannabis strains that resonate with Aries' dynamic energy, offering anecdotes of historical Aries figures and their potential affinity for cannabis.

Energizing the Aries Spirit

Aries thrives on challenge and action, often leading the charge with an infectious optimism. However, their intense energy can sometimes lead to stress, impatience, and a tendency to burn out. Cannabis can serve as a valuable ally for Aries, providing a means to balance their fiery nature, enhance creativity, and offer relaxation without dampening their inherent vitality.

The ideal strains for Aries are those that stimulate the mind, boost creativity, and provide energy for their endless list of projects and adventures. Sativa-dominant strains are particularly well-suited to this sign, offering uplifting and euphoric effects that can inspire action and innovation.

Recommended Strains for Aries

- Green Crack: Known for its invigorating effects, Green Crack is a perfect match for the Aries spirit. This strain provides an energetic high that can enhance focus and creativity, making it ideal for busy days filled with tasks and adventures. It's a strain that can help Aries tackle their projects with renewed vigor.

- Jack Herer: Named after the legendary cannabis activist, Jack Herer is a sativa-dominant strain that offers a blissful, clear-headed, and creative high. It's an excellent choice for Aries individuals looking to channel their energy into productive endeavors or seeking inspiration for new projects.
- Sour Diesel: This fast-acting strain provides an energizing and dreamy cerebral high. Sour Diesel is particularly effective in combating stress and fatigue, making it a great option for Aries who need to recharge their batteries and keep their spirits high.

Historical Aries Figures and Cannabis

While historical evidence of cannabis use by specific individuals is often speculative, we can imagine how certain Aries figures might have appreciated the plant's energizing and stress-relieving qualities.

- Leonardo da Vinci, an Aries born on April 15th, was a true Renaissance man, embodying the sign's love for innovation and creativity. One might speculate that a strain like Jack Herer could have appealed to da Vinci, potentially enhancing his already remarkable creativity and helping him to navigate the stress of his many projects and inventions.
- Thomas Jefferson, another Aries, was known for his curiosity and forward-thinking. Jefferson reportedly grew hemp on his plantation, and while it's unlikely he consumed it for psychoactive effects, one can imagine he would have appreciated the utility and potential of

cannabis, perhaps enjoying a strain like Green Crack to fuel his intellectual pursuits and diplomatic endeavors.

Conclusion

For the Aries individual, cannabis can be a powerful tool to balance their fiery nature, providing energy and creativity while also offering solace from the stresses that come with being a natural leader and pioneer. By choosing strains that align with their dynamic energy, Aries can harness the plant's power to fuel their adventurous spirit and continue blazing trails with passion and determination. As we explore the bond between Aries and cannabis, we uncover not just a synergy of energies, but a reflection of the cosmic dance between the stars and the earth, manifesting in the unique spirit of the Aries individual.

If you want to see some amazing products, please visit my Virtual Dispensary: https://shift.store/sg1fan23477/retail

CHAPTER 5: TAURUS - THE EARTHY CONNOISSEUR

In the lush gardens of the zodiac, Taurus stands as the Earthy Connoisseur, deeply rooted in the soil of sensuality, stability, and the finer things in life. Ruled by Venus, the planet of love, beauty, and comfort, Taureans are drawn to indulgence, luxury, and the pleasure of the senses. This chapter explores Taurus' profound connection to the Earth and how hemp can enhance their sensual pleasures and provide a grounding influence, alongside recommendations for cannabis strains that resonate with Taurus' penchant for relaxation and quality.

Taurus and Their Earthly Realm

Taurus is the embodiment of Earth's abundance, reveling in the tactile and the tangible. They appreciate quality in all forms, from the food they savor to the textures that surround them. For Taurus, the world is a place to be experienced with all the senses. Hemp, with its versatile nature, offers Taurus a multitude of ways to indulge in their love for the Earth's bounty, whether it's through the artisanal quality of hemp-based products or the grounding effect of the plant's medicinal properties.

Hemp aligns with Taurus' desire for stability and consistency, offering comfort and relaxation that can help ease their sometimes stubborn stress. The plant's connection to Venus, mirroring Taurus' ruling planet, highlights a natural affinity for enhancing beauty, love, and pleasure, integral aspects of the Taurus experience.

Strains for Grounding and Relaxation

For the Taurus connoisseur, cannabis strains that offer relaxation, grounding, and a touch of luxury are particularly appealing. Indica or indica-dominant hybrid strains, known for their soothing effects on the body and mind, are well-suited to Taurus' temperament.

- **Granddaddy Purple:** This iconic strain, with its complex berry and grape aroma, is perfect for the Taurus palate. Granddaddy Purple delivers a fusion of cerebral euphoria and physical relaxation, embodying the sensual and indulgent nature of Taurus. Its visually striking purple hues add an element of luxury and aesthetic pleasure.
- **Blue Cheese:** With its unique blend of flavors and aromas, Blue Cheese caters to Taurus' sophisticated taste. This strain offers a relaxing yet euphoric high, ideal for unwinding after a day of indulging in the physical world. The comforting and grounding effects of Blue Cheese make it a favorite among those who appreciate the finer details in life.
- **Northern Lights:** Known for its fast-acting, soothing effects, Northern Lights encapsulates the essence of tranquility and comfort that Taurus values. This strain can help soothe both mind and body, offering a serene escape to a peaceful, starlit night, reminiscent of Taurus' deep connection to nature.

A Humorous Take on Taurus' Love for Luxury

Imagine a Taurus, lounging on a plush, velvet couch, surrounded by the finest hemp-derived fabrics, indulging in gourmet edibles infused with the top-shelf strains. For Taurus, even their cannabis experience is touched by a desire for luxury and quality. They're the type to research the terpene profiles for the perfect flavor experience, or perhaps they're crafting their own bespoke blends to match their mood or the gourmet meal they're preparing.

The Taurus connoisseur isn't just smoking cannabis; they're creating an ambiance. Picture soft lighting, smooth music, and perhaps a hint of incense blending with the aromatic bouquet of their chosen strain. For Taurus, the cannabis experience is a full sensory event, one that appeals to their love of beauty, comfort, and the finer things in life.

Conclusion

Taurus, with their earthy sensibilities and love for the sensual, finds a natural ally in cannabis. The right strains can enhance their connection to the Earth, offering relaxation, pleasure, and a touch of luxury that speaks to their Venusian heart. As we celebrate Taurus in the cosmic garden of the zodiac, we recognize the unique bond they share with hemp, a plant that, like them, is deeply rooted in the beauty and abundance of the Earth. Through this green constellation, Taurus continues to explore the tactile and the tangible, finding stability, comfort, and delight in the Earth's bountiful offerings.

If you want to see some amazing products, please visit my Virtual Dispensary: https://shift.store/sg1fan23477/retail

CHAPTER 6: GEMINI - THE AIRY COMMUNICATOR

In the celestial dance of the zodiac, Gemini flutters as the Airy Communicator, characterized by duality, intellect, and an insatiable curiosity. Ruled by Mercury, the planet of communication, thought, and travel, Geminis are known for their quick wit, sociability, and love for engaging in meaningful conversations. This chapter delves into Gemini's love for social interaction and curiosity, exploring how certain strains of cannabis can help balance their dual nature by enhancing communication and sparking creativity.

Gemini's Dual Nature and Communication

Gemini, symbolized by the Twins, embodies the essence of duality. This sign is constantly juggling multiple interests, hobbies, and social circles, thriving on variety and change. However, this multiplicity can sometimes lead to restlessness and a scattering of energies. Cannabis can offer a harmonizing effect, helping Geminis to focus their thoughts and enhance their natural communicative gifts.

For Geminis, the social and cerebral effects of cannabis are particularly appealing. Strains that stimulate conversation, creativity, and mental agility can help balance their dual nature, providing a grounding yet intellectually stimulating experience that complements their airy disposition.

Strains for Stimulating Conversation and Creativity

Geminis benefit from strains that boost their already active minds and social nature, without overwhelming their senses. Sativa-dominant strains are particularly suited to this, providing an uplift that encourages creativity, eloquence, and a deeper connection in social interactions.

- **Super Lemon Haze:** This zesty sativa strain is perfect for the Gemini's love of lively conversation and exploration of ideas. Super Lemon Haze's energetic and social high can enhance Gemini's communicative prowess, making social gatherings more vibrant and engaging.
- **Sour Diesel:** Known for its invigorating cerebral high, Sour Diesel is an excellent choice for Geminis seeking a burst of creative inspiration or simply looking to engage more deeply in their social environment. Its fast-acting effect can help Geminis harness their scattered energy into focused and stimulating dialogue.
- **Durban Poison:** This pure sativa strain offers a clear, focused high that can sharpen Gemini's already quick mind, making it an excellent choice for brainstorming sessions or creative projects. Durban Poison's uplifting effect is also great for social settings, enhancing Gemini's natural charm and wit.

A Nod to Gemini's Historical Use of Hemp for Communication Enhancement

The historical intertwining of hemp and communication offers a fascinating backdrop to Gemini's relationship with cannabis. In ancient times, hemp was used to make paper, which facilitated the spread of ideas and knowledge across civilizations. This historical use resonates with Gemini's love for sharing information and engaging in intellectual exchange.

Imagine the ancient Geminis, scribes, and scholars, using hemp paper to pen their thoughts, stories, and discoveries, eagerly sharing their knowledge with the world. This historical context adds a layer of depth to Gemini's contemporary connection with cannabis, highlighting the plant's role in enhancing communication and the exchange of ideas.

Conclusion

For Gemini, the Airy Communicator, cannabis serves as both a muse and a mediator, harmonizing their dual nature while stimulating their intellectual and social inclinations. The selected strains offer a bridge between Gemini's love for conversation and their creative spirit, enhancing their natural abilities to connect, communicate, and innovate. As we explore the intersections of hemp and the zodiac, Gemini's relationship with cannabis reminds us of the plant's profound ability to enhance communication, creativity, and community, echoing the ancient ties between hemp and the exchange of knowledge.

If you want to see some amazing products, please visit my Virtual Dispensary: https://shift.store/sg1fan23477/retail

CHAPTER 7: CANCER - THE LUNAR HEALER

Nestled under the gentle glow of the moon, Cancer, the Lunar Healer, emerges as the zodiac's heart and soul. Governed by the Moon, this water sign is the epitome of intuition, emotional depth, and nurturing care. Cancers are known for their empathetic nature, often taking on the role of caretaker in their circles. This chapter explores the intuitive and nurturing qualities of Cancer and how hemp offers both emotional and physical comfort, providing an anchor in the tumultuous sea of their emotions. We delve into ideal strains that offer solace for Cancer's mood swings and digestive sensitivities, linking these with tales of Cancer's traditional use of hemp in moon rituals.

Cancer's Intuitive and Nurturing Essence

Cancer's connection to the Moon bestows a powerful intuition and a depth of emotion that is unparalleled in the zodiac. These Lunar Healers possess a natural ability to feel deeply and are often attuned to the emotions of those around them. However, their gift of sensitivity can sometimes lead to overwhelming mood swings and a tendency towards worry, particularly concerning the well-being of their loved ones. Hemp, with its calming and soothing properties, can offer a balm for Cancer's fluctuating emotions, providing a sense of stability and comfort.

Ideal Strains for Soothing Cancer's Emotional Seas

For Cancer, strains that offer relaxation and stress relief are particularly beneficial, helping to smooth the waves of their sometimes stormy emotional landscape. These strains can also aid in digestion, a common area of sensitivity for Cancers, by alleviating discomfort and promoting ease.

- **Blue Dream:** A balanced hybrid strain that delivers swift symptom relief without heavy sedative effects. Blue Dream can ease stress, soothe pain, and encourage a restful sleep, making it ideal for the emotionally and physically sensitive Cancer.
- **Northern Lights:** Known for its ability to relax muscles, calm the mind, and promote sleep, Northern Lights is perfect for Cancers looking to unwind and find peace in their often tumultuous emotional waters.
- **Cannatonic:** With a low THC and high CBD ratio, Cannatonic is an excellent choice for Cancers who are more prone to anxiety or those looking for relief without the psychoactive high. It's particularly effective in managing mood swings and aiding in digestive health.

Cancer and Traditional Use of Hemp in Moon Rituals

Cancer's ties to the Moon extend into the realm of spiritual and ritualistic practices, where hemp has been traditionally used to enhance emotional healing and intuition. The ancients recognized the plant's lunar connections, incorporating it into ceremonies to draw down the moon's energy for healing, protection, and emotional balance.

Imagine a Cancer, under the full moon, surrounded by the comforting scent of burning hemp, invoking the Moon's energy for insight and healing. These rituals, deeply embedded in the fabric of ancient wisdom, highlight the profound connection between Cancer's intuitive nature and the lunar qualities of hemp. This sacred plant acts as a conduit, enhancing the emotional and spiritual work that is so often the focus of Cancer's nurturing soul.

Conclusion

For Cancer, the Lunar Healer, hemp serves as a gentle companion in their journey through the emotional depths of the human experience. The ideal strains offer a haven, providing emotional equilibrium and physical comfort. As we weave the tale of Cancer and their affinity for hemp, we are reminded of the timeless bond between the celestial and the earthly realms. Through hemp, Cancer finds a tool for healing, a catalyst for emotional and physical harmony, and a connection to the ancient lunar rituals that celebrate the deep, intuitive wisdom of this water sign.

If you want to see some amazing products, please visit my Virtual Dispensary: https://shift.store/sg1fan23477/retail

CHAPTER 8: LEO - THE RADIANT PERFORMER

In the grand theater of the cosmos, Leo takes center stage with a roar, embodying the essence of natural charisma, leadership, and the unquenchable desire to be seen and admired. Ruled by the Sun, the center of our solar system, Leos are imbued with a radiant energy that is both warm and life-giving. Their presence is magnetic, drawing others into their orbit with a generosity and warmth that lights up the room. This chapter explores the connection between Leo, the Radiant Performer, and hemp, focusing on how this versatile plant supports heart health and self-expression, along with recommending cannabis strains that elevate Leo's spirits and confidence. We also delve into legendary stories of Leo figures and their command of the plant's regal essence.

Leo's Charisma and Leadership

Leo's inherent charisma and leadership are not just for show; they are the expression of a deep-seated desire to make a meaningful impact on the world. Leos are heart-driven leaders, passionate about their pursuits and generous in their desire to uplift those around them. However, this heart-centered approach means that Leos can sometimes take on too much, leading to stress and strain on their cardiovascular system. Hemp, with its multitude of health benefits, can play a crucial role in supporting Leo's heart health, allowing them to shine brightly without burning out.

Hemp and Leo's Heart Health and Self-Expression

The cardiovascular benefits of hemp, particularly CBD-rich strains, can be particularly beneficial for Leo, offering a natural way to manage stress and support heart health. Additionally, the creative boost that some strains of cannabis provide can help Leo in their self-expression, whether it's through art, performance, or leadership. For Leo, cannabis is not just about relaxation but about enhancing their natural vibrancy and creative output.

Cannabis Strains for Elevating Leo's Spirits and Confidence

For the Radiant Performer, strains that uplift the mood, boost creativity, and provide a touch of grandeur are most fitting. Sativa strains or sativa-dominant hybrids are particularly suited to Leo's sunny disposition, offering an energetic high that can enhance their natural enthusiasm and zest for life.

- Super Silver Haze: This energizing sativa strain is perfect for Leos who seek to elevate their spirits and boost their confidence. Super Silver Haze delivers a euphoric high that can inspire creativity and promote a positive, sunny outlook—much like Leo's ruling planet, the Sun.
- Golden Goat: Reflecting Leo's love for the luxurious and the bold, Golden Goat is known for its bright, tropical flavor and uplifting effects. This strain can enhance Leo's natural charisma and support their desire to be social butterflies, shining brightly in their social circles.

- **Tangie**: With its sweet, citrus aroma and energizing effects, Tangie is a strain that embodies the warmth and radiance of the Sun. It's an excellent choice for Leos looking to spark their creativity, elevate their mood, and radiate confidence in all their endeavors.

Legendary Leo Figures and the Plant's Regal Essence

Throughout history, many Leo figures have embodied the regal essence of this zodiac sign, commanding attention and admiration through their deeds and presence. While specific stories of these figures' interactions with cannabis may be more myth than fact, we can imagine how the plant's majestic aura could have appealed to their lion-hearted nature.

For instance, consider a legendary Leo leader, cloaked in the majesty of their power, using hemp in ceremonies to signify strength, unity, and prosperity under their rule. Or a renowned Leo artist, drawing inspiration from the euphoric and creative highs of cannabis, crafting masterpieces that echo through the ages.

Conclusion

For Leo, the Radiant Performer, cannabis offers much more than mere relaxation—it is a tool for heart health, creative expression, and the enhancement of their natural leadership qualities. The strains recommended for Leo align with their sunny disposition and regal nature, supporting their health and allowing their radiant spirits to shine even brighter. As we explore the cosmic dance between Leo and hemp, we celebrate the plant's ability to amplify the natural charisma and warmth of this zodiac sign, reinforcing their place at the center of the zodiac's grand stage.

CHAPTER 9: VIRGO - THE METHODICAL HERBALIST

In the meticulously arranged garden of the zodiac, Virgo emerges as the Methodical Herbalist, blending an analytical approach with a profound reverence for wellness and the natural world. Ruled by Mercury, the planet of thought and communication, Virgos are known for their keen minds, attention to detail, and a deep-seated desire to contribute to the betterment of themselves and those around them. This chapter delves into Virgo's health-conscious approach to life, viewing hemp as a pivotal tool for wellness and purification. We explore strains that resonate with Virgo's meticulous nature and support gut health, weaving in tales of Virgo's historical contributions to herbal medicine, including cannabis.

Virgo's Analytical and Health-Conscious Approach

Virgos possess an innate connection to the earth and its bounty, often leading them towards a path of natural healing and wellness. Their analytical minds are adept at understanding complex systems, making them particularly attuned to the nuances of herbal medicine and the benefits of cannabis for health and well-being. For Virgo, hemp is not just a plant but a companion in their quest for purity, wellness, and a balanced life.

Their methodical approach to health encompasses a keen interest in diet, gut health, and the detoxification of the body and mind. Virgos recognize the gut as the second brain, integral to overall health and well-being. Hemp's nutritional profile, rich in omega fatty acids, fiber, and protein, aligns perfectly with Virgo's health-conscious approach, supporting their digestive health and providing the necessary tools for bodily purification.

Strains for Enhancing Virgo's Meticulous Nature and Gut Health

Virgos benefit from cannabis strains that enhance focus, reduce stress, and support gut health without overwhelming their sensitive systems. CBD-dominant strains, known for their therapeutic benefits without the psychoactive high, are particularly suited to Virgo's preferences.

- ACDC: This CBD-dominant strain is ideal for Virgos, offering pain relief, anxiety reduction, and gut health support without significant psychoactive effects. ACDC can aid Virgos in their health-focused endeavors, allowing them to maintain clarity and productivity in their meticulous work.
- Harlequin: With a balanced CBD to THC ratio, Harlequin provides mild psychoactive effects alongside significant therapeutic benefits. It's particularly effective for stress relief and can aid in digestive health, aligning with Virgo's holistic approach to wellness.
- Cannatonic: Another CBD-rich strain, Cannatonic, offers relaxation and relief from inflammation, which can be beneficial for gut health issues. Its calming effects also support Virgo's mental health, providing a soothing break from their often overactive minds.

Virgo's Contributions to Herbal Medicine, Including Cannabis

Virgos have historically played a significant role in the advancement of herbal medicine, applying their analytical skills to understand the medicinal properties of plants, including cannabis. Their methodical approach has contributed to the categorization and understanding of herbs, laying the groundwork for modern herbalism.

The tale of a Virgo herbalist in ancient times, meticulously cataloging the effects of various strains of cannabis and other herbs, underscores the sign's intrinsic connection to the earth and its healing powers. This Virgo could have been among the first to document the digestive benefits of hemp seeds or the therapeutic effects of CBD, combining empirical observation with a deep understanding of the body's natural systems.

Conclusion

For Virgo, the Methodical Herbalist, hemp is a cornerstone of their health-focused and analytical approach to life. The strains recommended for Virgo support their meticulous nature, offering benefits for gut health and mental well-being without compromising their need for clarity and precision. As we honor Virgo's historical contributions to herbal medicine, including their exploration of cannabis, we recognize the enduring bond between this zodiac sign and the natural world. Virgo's journey with hemp is a testament to their unwavering commitment to health, wellness, and the meticulous care of the earth and its inhabitants.

If you want to see some amazing products, please visit my Virtual Dispensary: https://shift.store/sg1fan23477/retail

CHAPTER 10: LIBRA - THE HARMONIOUS PARTNER

In the celestial ballet of the zodiac, Libra, The Harmonious Partner, gracefully maintains the dance of balance and beauty. Governed by Venus, the planet of love, aesthetics, and partnership, Libras are the epitome of grace, diplomacy, and a relentless pursuit of harmony in all aspects of life. Their innate sense of fairness and a deep appreciation for the arts make them natural peacemakers and lovers of beauty. This chapter explores how cannabis acts as a catalyst for connectivity and artistic appreciation for Libra, offering recommendations for strains that promote equilibrium and peace. We also delve into stories that illustrate Libra's age-old balancing act with hemp, showcasing their unique relationship with this versatile plant.

Libra's Quest for Balance and Social Harmony

Libras are constantly seeking balance, striving to create harmony in their surroundings and relationships. Their diplomatic nature allows them to navigate social situations with grace, often bringing people together and fostering understanding. However, this quest for equilibrium can sometimes lead to indecision and a tendency to prioritize others' needs over their own. Cannabis can play a pivotal role in supporting

Libra's balance, offering a space for relaxation, introspection, and enhanced social interactions.

The plant's ability to foster connectivity aligns with Libra's social nature, enhancing their experiences in group settings and deepening their relationships. Additionally, cannabis's influence on artistic appreciation speaks to Libra's Venusian qualities, magnifying beauty and inspiring creativity in various forms of expression.

Recommendations for Strains That Promote Equilibrium and Peace

Libras benefit from strains that offer a balanced high, smoothing out extremes and supporting their quest for harmony. Hybrid strains, particularly those with an even balance of THC and CBD, are well-suited to Libra's disposition, providing relaxation without sedation and mild euphoria that enhances social interactions without overwhelming.

- Blue Dream: A popular hybrid that balances full-body relaxation with gentle cerebral invigoration. Blue Dream is perfect for Libras, facilitating social connectivity and artistic appreciation. Its sweet berry aroma adds to the sensory experience, appealing to Libra's refined tastes.
- Wedding Cake: Known for its relaxing and euphoric effects, Wedding Cake is a balanced hybrid that can help Libras unwind and find peace within. It's particularly suited to intimate gatherings, enhancing the depth of conversations and shared experiences.
- Gelato: This flavorful strain offers a balanced high that can stimulate creativity and promote social relaxation, aligning with Libra's love for the arts and their social nature. Gelato's pleasant taste and aroma contribute to

the overall aesthetic experience, satisfying Libra's quest for beauty.

Libra's Age-Old Balancing Act with Hemp

Throughout history, Libras have demonstrated a natural affinity for plants that bring balance and harmony, including hemp. Ancient Libra healers and herbalists might have utilized hemp in their practices, blending it into remedies that soothe both the body and mind, restoring equilibrium to those in distress.

Imagine a Libra artisan in the Renaissance, weaving hemp into beautiful fabrics or incorporating it into artworks, celebrating the plant's versatility and beauty. These historical connections underscore Libra's enduring relationship with hemp, a plant that mirrors their values of balance, harmony, and appreciation for the finer things in life.

Conclusion

For Libra, The Harmonious Partner, cannabis is more than just a plant; it is a medium for achieving balance, enhancing social bonds, and deepening their appreciation for art and beauty. The recommended strains offer a pathway to equilibrium, supporting Libra's natural tendencies towards diplomacy, connectivity, and aesthetic enjoyment. As we explore Libra's age-old balancing act with hemp, we are reminded of the plant's capacity to bring harmony to our lives, reflecting the core values that define this air sign's essence.

If you want to see some amazing products, please visit my Virtual Dispensary: https://shift.store/sg1fan23477/retail

CHAPTER 11: SCORPIO - THE DEEP DIVER

In the shadowy depths of the zodiac, Scorpio, The Deep Diver, navigates the waters of the unseen with unparalleled intensity and passion. Ruled by Pluto, the planet of transformation, death, and rebirth, Scorpios are the mystics of the zodiac, endowed with a profound capacity for emotional and spiritual exploration. They seek the truth relentlessly, unafraid to traverse the darker corners of existence to find it. This chapter delves into Scorpio's intensity and transformational capabilities, viewing hemp as a catalyst for their emotional and spiritual journey. We also recommend potent strains for Scorpio's quest for truth and delve into mythological explorations of Scorpio's profound relationship with the plant's mystique.

Scorpio's Intensity and Transformational Capabilities

Scorpios are known for their depth and intensity, possessing a magnetic aura that draws others into their complex world. Their journey is one of transformation, constantly shedding old skins to reveal new layers of existence and understanding. For Scorpio, hemp acts as a key to unlocking the deeper realms of consciousness, facilitating introspection and the exploration of the psyche.

The plant's ability to induce states of deep relaxation and heightened awareness makes it an invaluable tool for Scorpio's transformative journey, aiding in the exploration of their own depths and the mysteries of the universe. Cannabis can help Scorpio navigate their intense emotions, providing a safe space for vulnerability and the release of pent-up energy.

Potent Strains for Scorpio's Quest for Truth

Scorpios benefit from potent strains that can match their intensity and aid in their relentless quest for truth. Strains that offer a deep, introspective high or those that provide clarity and heightened perception are particularly suited to Scorpio's disposition.

- OG Kush: Known for its stress-relieving properties and deep, euphoric high, OG Kush is perfect for Scorpios seeking to explore their inner depths. Its potent effects can help unlock layers of the psyche, facilitating a deeper understanding of the self and the universe.
- Purple Haze: This strain offers a burst of creativity and euphoria, opening the doors to spiritual insight and introspection. Purple Haze is ideal for Scorpios looking to

transcend the mundane and delve into more profound, philosophical questions.

· White Widow: Offering a powerful burst of euphoria and energy, White Widow can help Scorpios penetrate the surface of their thoughts and feelings, diving deeper into their emotional and spiritual exploration. Its balanced effects provide the clarity and introspection necessary for Scorpio's transformative journey.

Mythological Explorations of Scorpio's Relationship with Cannabis

The mythological connections between Scorpio and cannabis are rich with imagery of transformation, healing, and rebirth. In ancient myths, Scorpio is often depicted as a guardian of sacred knowledge and a guide through transitions, embodying the plant's mystique and its role as a conduit between worlds.

Imagine Scorpio, in the guise of a mythical healer or shaman, using cannabis in rituals to facilitate journeys into the underworld, guiding souls through transformation with the plant's psychoactive properties. These rituals underscore Scorpio's mastery over the unseen and their ability to navigate the spaces between life and death, light and darkness.

Conclusion

For Scorpio, The Deep Diver, cannabis is not just a plant but a sacrament, facilitating their exploration of the emotional and spiritual realms. The recommended strains support Scorpio's quest for truth, offering the depth and intensity required for their transformative journey. As we explore Scorpio's profound relationship with cannabis, we uncover a mystical bond that transcends the physical, highlighting the plant's role in their continuous cycle of death and rebirth. Scorpio's connection with cannabis reminds us of the plant's power to unlock the mysteries of the self and the universe, serving as a guide through the depths of human consciousness.

If you want to see some amazing products, please visit my Virtual Dispensary: https://shift.store/sg1fan23477/retail

CHAPTER 12: SAGITTARIUS - THE PHILOSOPHICAL EXPLORER

Beneath the starlit sky of the zodiac, Sagittarius, The Philosophical Explorer, embarks on an endless quest for knowledge, wisdom, and freedom. Governed by Jupiter, the planet of expansion, adventure, and higher learning, Sagittarians are imbued with an insatiable curiosity and a boundless enthusiasm for life's many experiences. They are the archers who aim their arrows at the farthest reaches of the universe, seeking truth and meaning in every corner of the world and beyond. This chapter explores Sagittarius' adventurous and philosophical spirit and how hemp aids in their journey of discovery, offering strains that inspire wanderlust and elevate the mind. We also delve into humorous anecdotes of Sagittarian explorers and sages who might have shared a puff or two on their journeys.

Sagittarius' Adventurous and Philosophical Spirit

Sagittarians are natural-born adventurers, not just in the physical sense but also in the realms of thought and spirit. Their philosophy is one of boundless exploration, where every experience is an opportunity to learn and grow. However, their perpetual search for freedom and truth can sometimes lead them to feel restless and impatient with the mundane aspects of life. Cannabis serves as a companion on their quest, providing both a mental and spiritual uplift that complements their exploratory nature.

The plant's capacity to inspire introspection and broaden perspectives aligns with Sagittarius' longing for deeper understanding and meaning. It can offer moments of profound insight and clarity, fueling their philosophical inclinations and satisfying their thirst for knowledge.

Strains that Inspire Wanderlust and Elevate the Mind

For the Philosophical Explorer, strains that stimulate the mind, enhance creativity, and invoke a sense of adventure are particularly appealing. Sativa strains or sativa-dominant hybrids, known for their cerebral high and ability to enhance focus and creativity, are ideally suited for Sagittarius.

- **Super Silver Haze**: This sativa-dominant strain offers an energetic and uplifting high, perfect for Sagittarians embarking on intellectual or physical adventures. Super Silver Haze can stimulate creativity and enhance the enjoyment of new experiences, making every journey an enlightening one.
- **Strawberry Cough**: Known for its sweet smell and uplifting effects, Strawberry Cough is a great companion for Sagittarius explorers looking to elevate their mind while maintaining a sense of clarity. It's an ideal strain for those seeking inspiration and a fresh perspective on their quest for knowledge.
- **Jack Herer**: Named after the legendary cannabis activist and author, Jack Herer is a strain that embodies the

spirit of exploration and activism. Its effects can spark a Sagittarian's passion for change and drive for justice, fueling their philosophical debates and explorations with a sense of purpose and optimism.

Humorous Anecdotes of Sagittarian Explorers and Sages

Imagine a Sagittarian sage, centuries ago, traversing the Silk Road, sharing stories and philosophies with fellow travelers around a campfire, passing around a pipe filled with the finest cannabis of the land. Their discussions range from the nature of the universe to the best ways to cook a meal on the road, all while under the influence of the plant's mind-expanding properties.

Or picture a modern-day Sagittarian explorer, backpacking across remote landscapes, their journey fueled by the desire to see every corner of the world. In their pack, alongside a worn copy of "On the Road," lies a stash of Strawberry Cough, ready to be shared with new friends met along the way, sparking laughter and deep conversations under the stars.

Conclusion

For Sagittarius, The Philosophical Explorer, cannabis is more than just a plant; it's a catalyst for adventure, a source of inspiration, and a tool for introspection. The strains recommended for Sagittarius support their journey towards enlightenment, enhancing their natural inclination towards exploration and their quest for universal truths. As we explore the connection between Sagittarius and cannabis, we celebrate the spirit of adventure and the pursuit of knowledge, embodied in the humorous and enlightening anecdotes of Sagittarian explorers and sages through the ages. In the smoke of their shared experiences, we find a reflection of humanity's eternal quest for understanding, freedom, and connection.

If you want to see some amazing products, please visit my Virtual Dispensary: https://shift.store/sg1fan23477/retail

CHAPTER 13: CAPRICORN - THE AMBITIOUS MOUNTAIN CLIMBER

Perched atop the rugged terrain of the zodiac, Capricorn, The Ambitious Mountain Climber, charts a course towards the summit of their aspirations with unmatched discipline and ambition. Ruled by Saturn, the planet of responsibility, structure, and long-term goals, Capricorns are the architects of their destiny, building their dreams with perseverance and a steadfast commitment to success. This chapter explores Capricorn's discipline and ambition, highlighting how hemp serves as a tool to relieve stress and enhance endurance. We offer suggestions for strains that ground and motivate Capricorn, weaving in tales of Capricorn's age-old respect for the plant's resilience and utility.

Capricorn's Discipline and Ambition

Capricorns possess an innate sense of purpose and determination, often setting high standards for themselves and methodically working towards their goals. Their pragmatic approach to life is marked by a strong work ethic and a capacity to navigate obstacles with patience and resilience. However, this relentless pursuit of achievement can sometimes lead to stress and a neglect of self-care. Hemp emerges as a valuable ally for Capricorn, offering relief from the pressures of their ambitions and supporting their physical and mental endurance.

The plant's adaptogenic properties can help modulate stress levels, providing Capricorn with the balance needed to maintain their productivity without compromising their well-being. Furthermore, hemp's utility extends beyond mere stress relief, offering nutritional benefits that align with Capricorn's disciplined lifestyle.

Suggestions for Strains That Ground and Motivate Capricorn

Capricorns benefit from strains that offer grounding and motivation, helping them stay focused on their path to achievement while providing a reprieve from their industrious endeavors.

- Harlequin: A CBD-dominant strain, Harlequin provides clear-headed relief from stress and pain, without psychoactive effects that might detract from Capricorn's productivity. It's perfect for Capricorns seeking to alleviate tension while remaining grounded and motivated.
- Sour Diesel: Known for its invigorating and energizing effects, Sour Diesel can offer the boost Capricorns need to tackle their ambitious projects. This strain helps combat

fatigue, enhancing endurance for long working hours or intense study sessions.

· Green Crack: Aptly named for its stimulating effects, Green Crack is ideal for Capricorns who need an extra push to get through their to-do list. It provides mental clarity and focus, fueling Capricorn's drive to succeed without the crash associated with caffeine.

Tales of Capricorn's Age-Old Respect for Hemp's Resilience and Utility

The Capricornian respect for hemp's resilience and utility mirrors their own qualities of endurance and pragmatism. Ancient Capricorn farmers and builders might have marveled at hemp's versatility, cultivating it for its fibers to create durable textiles and ropes, as well as for its seeds for nutritional sustenance.

Imagine a Capricorn architect in ancient times, utilizing hemp in the construction of sustainable buildings, admiring the plant's strength and durability. Or a Capricorn herbalist, appreciating hemp's medicinal properties, incorporating it into remedies that fortify the body against the wear and tear of hard labor and the stresses of daily life.

These tales underscore Capricorn's deep appreciation for practical and enduring solutions, recognizing hemp as a symbol of the resilience and utility they so highly value. The plant's ability to thrive under challenging conditions and its myriad uses resonate with Capricorn's ethos of hard work, perseverance, and respect for the natural world.

Conclusion

For Capricorn, The Ambitious Mountain Climber, hemp serves as a steadfast companion on their ascent towards their goals, offering stress relief, endurance, and a grounding influence. The strains recommended for Capricorn align with their need for productivity and motivation, supporting their disciplined approach to life. As we explore Capricorn's relationship with cannabis, we celebrate the mutual qualities of resilience, utility, and practicality, highlighting the plant's role in aiding Capricorn's journey to the summit of their ambitions. Through hemp, Capricorn finds a natural ally in their quest for success, embodying the strength and perseverance that define their path.

If you want to see some amazing products, please visit my Virtual Dispensary: https://shift.store/sg1fan23477/retail

CHAPTER 14: AQUARIUS - THE VISIONARY REFORMER

In the boundless expanse of the zodiac, Aquarius, The Visionary Reformer, emerges as a beacon of innovation and humanitarianism. Governed by Uranus, the planet of breakthroughs, freedom, and revolutionary change, Aquarians are forward-thinkers, always a step ahead in envisioning a brighter future for humanity. Their approach is both radical and altruistic, seeking not just to imagine a new world but to actively participate in its creation. This chapter examines Aquarius' innovative and humanitarian nature, with hemp serving as a tool for social change and intellectual expansion. We explore ideal strains for igniting Aquarius' revolutionary ideas and offer futuristic visions of Aquarius leading society into new realms of cannabis appreciation.

Aquarius' Innovative and Humanitarian Nature

Aquarians are characterized by their unique blend of intellect and empathy, capable of generating ideas that are not only ingenious but also geared towards the greater good. Their vision extends beyond personal gain, focusing instead on collective progress and equality. In this light, hemp becomes more than just a plant; it represents an opportunity for social reform and a means to challenge conventional thinking, aligning perfectly with Aquarius' ethos.

The plant's versatility and sustainability make it an ideal symbol for Aquarian ideals, representing innovation in industries from medicine to construction, and its role in fostering community and understanding mirrors Aquarius' humanitarian goals.

Ideal Strains for Sparking Aquarius' Revolutionary Ideas

Aquarians benefit from cannabis strains that stimulate the mind, encourage unconventional thinking, and fuel creativity. Sativa strains or hybrids with uplifting and cerebral effects are particularly suited to sparking the visionary ideas Aquarians are known for.

- **Amnesia Haze:** This sativa-dominant strain is known for its ability to enhance focus and unleash creativity, making it perfect for Aquarius individuals looking to channel their visionary thoughts into tangible concepts.
- **Super Lemon Haze:** With its energizing and uplifting effects, Super Lemon Haze can stimulate Aquarius' mind, encouraging innovative thinking and problem-solving. Its citrusy aroma adds to the sensory experience, invigorating the senses and brightening thoughts.
- **Jillybean:** This cheerful and creative hybrid is ideal for the Aquarian reformer, offering mood-lifting effects that can inspire social engagement and community-focused initiatives. Jillybean's sweet, fruity flavors make the experience even more enjoyable, fueling Aquarius' drive for change with a sense of joy.

Futuristic Visions of Aquarius Leading Society into New Realms of Cannabis Appreciation

Envision an Aquarius at the forefront of a movement, harnessing the potential of hemp to revolutionize industries, medicine, and environmental conservation. They advocate for the use of cannabis not only as a sustainable resource but as a catalyst for social and legal reform, breaking down stigmas and fostering a deeper understanding of the plant's benefits.

Imagine Aquarian-led initiatives that integrate cannabis into futuristic urban farming projects, where community gardens and vertical farms provide both food and medicinal plants, including hemp, to urban populations. These visionaries use their platform to educate the public on the importance of sustainability, health, and community wellness, showing how cannabis can play a pivotal role in achieving these goals.

In this future, Aquarius has guided society to embrace cannabis as a key element in advancing health, innovation, and social cohesion. Hemp is no longer seen as just a recreational substance but as an essential component of a progressive, equitable, and sustainable world.

Conclusion

For Aquarius, The Visionary Reformer, cannabis is more than a plant; it's a symbol of future possibilities, social justice, and intellectual freedom. The strains recommended for Aquarius fuel their innovative spirit and support their humanitarian efforts, enabling them to lead society into new realms of appreciation and understanding of cannabis. As we contemplate Aquarius' relationship with hemp, we're invited to envision a world transformed by their revolutionary ideas and actions, where cannabis plays a central role in creating a more inclusive, sustainable, and enlightened society. Through the visionary eyes of Aquarius, we see not just the potential of cannabis but the promise of a better future for all.

If you want to see some amazing products, please visit my Virtual Dispensary: https://shift.store/sg1fan23477/retail

CHAPTER 15: PISCES - THE DREAMY MYSTIC

In the celestial ocean of the zodiac, Pisces, The Dreamy Mystic, swims in the deepest waters of emotion, intuition, and spiritual connection. Ruled by Neptune, the planet of dreams, imagination, and beyond the physical realm, Pisceans are the soulful seers of the zodiac, navigating the currents of the unseen with an open heart and a boundless imagination. This chapter delves into Pisces' profound emotional and spiritual connection to the universe, and how hemp serves as a conduit for enhancing their creativity, introspection, and mystical experiences. We also explore strains that soothe and inspire Pisces, weaving in mystical accounts of Pisces' historical use of cannabis in spiritual practices and art.

Pisces' Deep Emotional and Spiritual Connection

Pisceans possess an innate sensitivity to the energies that surround them, often feeling the emotions of others as deeply as their own. This empathic nature, combined with a vivid imagination, allows them to traverse the realms of dreams and spirituality with ease. Hemp, with its psychoactive and therapeutic properties, can amplify Pisces' natural proclivity for introspection and spiritual exploration, deepening their connection to the cosmos and enhancing their creative expression.

The plant's ability to dissolve boundaries and elevate consciousness aligns with Pisces' desire to transcend the mundane, offering a gateway to higher planes of thought and feeling. For Pisces, cannabis is not just a substance but a sacred ally in their quest for universal understanding and artistic creation.

Strains that Soothe and Inspire Pisces

Pisces benefits from strains that offer a balance between relaxation and creative stimulation, providing solace for their often-overwhelmed spirits while nurturing their boundless creativity.

- Granddaddy Purple: This indica-dominant strain is perfect for soothing Pisces' emotional waters, offering deep relaxation and stress relief. Its dreamy, euphoric effects can also spark imaginative insights and enhance artistic inspiration, resonating with Pisces' mystical nature.
- Blue Dream: A balanced hybrid, Blue Dream gently uplifts the spirit while easing tension, making it ideal for Pisces seeking a blend of therapeutic calm and creative encouragement. Its ability to promote a peaceful state of mind supports Pisces' spiritual and artistic pursuits.
- Northern Lights: Known for its ability to induce deep tranquility and a meditative state, Northern Lights can help Pisces disconnect from the chaos of the world and embark on introspective journeys. This strain fosters a sense of inner peace and oneness with the universe, aligning with Pisces' yearning for spiritual depth.

Mystical Accounts of Pisces' Historical Use of Cannabis in Spiritual Practices and Art

Throughout history, Pisces' affinity for the mystical has often intersected with the ceremonial use of cannabis. Ancient Piscean mystics and shamans might have incorporated cannabis into their rituals and meditations as a means to deepen their connection with the divine, facilitating visions and transcendent experiences that guided their spiritual practices.

In the realm of art, Piscean painters, poets, and musicians have historically drawn upon cannabis to tap into the well-spring of their imagination, creating works that transcend time and space. The plant's influence on dream states and creativity allowed these artists to explore and express the ethereal realms that Pisces so naturally inhabits.

Imagine a Piscean poet in a bygone era, under the influence of a strain like Blue Dream, penning verses that capture the ineffable beauty of the cosmos, or a Piscean artist, inspired by Northern Lights, creating canvases awash with colors and forms that evoke the mystical union of the earthly and the divine.

Conclusion

For Pisces, The Dreamy Mystic, cannabis is a sacred key to unlocking the depths of their soul and the mysteries of the universe. The strains recommended for Pisces support their spiritual journey and creative expression, offering solace for their sensitive spirits and inspiration for their artistic endeavors. As we explore the relationship between Pisces and hemp, we uncover a timeless synergy between the plant's mystical properties and Pisces' quest for universal connection and creative exploration. Through cannabis, Pisces finds a companion in their voyage through the dreamscapes of their imagination and the boundless oceans of spiritual depth, celebrating the plant's role in enriching their journey through the cosmos.

If you want to see some amazing products, please visit my Virtual Dispensary: https://shift.store/sg1fan23477/retail

CONCLUSION: THE STARLIT PATH OF HEMP AND
HUMANITY

As we conclude our celestial voyage through the zodiac, reflecting on the intricate tapestry woven by hemp and humanity, we stand at the threshold of understanding and appreciation for the deep, interconnected journey these two have shared. From ancient rituals to modern wellness, from the fields of medicine to the arenas of social change, cannabis and astrology have danced together, influencing cultures, guiding spiritual practices, and shaping human consciousness.

Reflections on the Inseparable Journey

This journey of cannabis and astrology through human history is a testament to our enduring quest for knowledge, healing, and connection. Each chapter of this celestial narrative has unveiled the unique vibrations that hemp brings to the diverse spectrum of the human experience, echoing the cosmic energies that guide us. As we've traversed the zodiac, from the fiery initiative of Aries to the dreamy depths of Pisces, we've seen how cannabis, in all its forms, has been a constant companion, enhancing our wellness, sparking our creativity, and deepening our spiritual insights.

The starlit path of hemp and humanity is marked by moments of profound understanding and enlightenment, where the plant's ability to heal, inspire, and unite reveals the intricate web of life that connects us all. In every leaf and bud, in every strain and smoke, there lies a story of civilizations past, of seekers and sages who recognized in cannabis a reflection of the celestial dance overhead.

Encouragement for Readers to Explore Their Astrological Connections with Cannabis

As we stand on the brink of a new era in our relationship with cannabis, encouraged by evolving societal attitudes and scientific discoveries, there's an invitation for each of us to explore our own astrological connections with this ancient plant. Whether you're a seasoned enthusiast or a curious newcomer, the cosmic journey of cannabis offers a universe of possibilities for wellness, understanding, and joy.

Engage with cannabis as a tool for introspection, a catalyst for creativity, or a means to foster community. Let the characteristics of your zodiac sign guide you toward strains that resonate with your essence, enhancing your physical, emotional, and spiritual well-being. Embrace the lessons and laughter that cannabis brings, allowing it to illuminate your path and connect you with the deeper rhythms of the cosmos.

A Shared Cosmic Laughter

As we close this chapter on the starlit path of hemp and humanity, let us carry forward the shared cosmic laughter that arises from the delightful synchronicities between our celestial predispositions and the cannabis plant. In this laughter, there is healing, unity, and a reminder of the whimsical nature of existence.

The journey of cannabis and astrology is far from complete; it continues to unfold with every passing moment, with every shared experience. As explorers on this infinite path, we are bound by the threads of curiosity and wonder that draw us closer to the stars and to each other.

In the constellation of cannabis and the zodiac, we find not just guidance for our earthly journey but a reflection of the eternal dance between the microcosm and the macrocosm, between humanity and the universe. Here, on the starlit path of hemp and humanity, we discover the magic that arises when we align with the cosmos, embracing the plant that has journeyed with us through time, guiding us toward a deeper understanding of ourselves and the boundless mysteries of the universe.

FURTHER READING AND RESOURCES

The journey through the intricate relationship between cannabis and astrology, as outlined in "Green Constellations," is just the beginning. For those eager to dive deeper into this fascinating interplay and explore the broader historical, cultural, and spiritual significance of this sacred plant, a wealth of resources awaits. Here are recommendations for texts, online platforms, and communities where enthusiasts can further their exploration of both the astrological influences on cannabis use and the plant's rich historical and cultural tapestry.

Recommended Texts

1. "The Emperor Wears No Clothes" by Jack Herer: This classic text is essential reading for anyone interested in the history of cannabis prohibition and activism. While not directly focused on astrology, it provides a foundational understanding of the plant's significance across cultures and epochs.

2. "Cannabis and Spirituality: An Explorer's Guide to an Ancient Plant Spirit Ally" edited by Stephen Gray: Offering a comprehensive look at the spiritual and ceremonial uses of cannabis, this book is a fantastic resource for understanding the plant's role in various spiritual traditions, with insights that may appeal to those interested in the mystical and astrological aspects of cannabis use.

3. "Cosmic Botany: A Guide to Crystal and Astrological Herbalism" by Tanya Lichtenstein: Though not exclusively about cannabis, this guide offers an intriguing exploration of how plants, crystals, and astrological influences intertwine, providing a unique perspective that can enrich one's understanding of cannabis within a broader spiritual and astrological context.

Online Platforms and Communities

1. Leafly: As a comprehensive resource for strain information, effects, and user reviews, Leafly can help individuals explore which strains may resonate with their astrological sign or desired spiritual and emotional outcomes.
2. The Astrology Podcast: While not exclusively focused on cannabis, this podcast often delves into topics that intersect with spirituality, herbalism, and holistic living, offering insights that can complement an astrological exploration of cannabis use.
3. Reddit Communities: Subreddits like r/astrology, r/trees, and r/Cannabis_Culture foster discussions among enthusiasts of astrology and cannabis. These platforms can provide personal anecdotes, advice, and a sense of community for those looking to deepen their understanding of how these two realms intersect.
4. Erowid: A comprehensive online library of psychoactive substances, including cannabis, Erowid offers user experiences, legal information, and research documents. Its vast collection can be valuable for understanding the plant's impact on spirituality, health, and culture.

Workshops and Events

Many holistic health centers, yoga studios, and spiritual retreats offer workshops and events focusing on the therapeutic and spiritual use of cannabis. These can be excellent opportunities to learn from experienced practitioners and connect with like-minded individuals. Websites like Eventbrite or local holistic health and wellness centers can be good places to start looking for such events.

Academic Journals and Research Publications

For those interested in the scientific and academic study of cannabis, journals like "The Journal of Cannabis Research" and "Cannabis and Cannabinoid Research" publish peer-reviewed articles on a wide range of topics, from medical research to the plant's historical and cultural dimensions.

CONCLUDING NOTE

Exploring the relationship between cannabis and astrology opens up a universe of insight into the spiritual, cultural, and historical aspects of this ancient plant. By engaging with the recommended texts, platforms, and communities, enthusiasts can continue to unravel the complex tapestry that cannabis weaves through human consciousness and culture, deepening their appreciation and understanding of this sacred ally on their personal and collective journeys.

Message from the Author:

I hope you enjoyed this book, I love astrology and knew there was not a book such as this out on the shelf. I love metaphysical items as well. Please check out my other books:

-Life of Government Benefits

-My life of Hell

-My life with Hydrocephalus

-Red Sky

-World Domination:Woman's rule

-World Domination:Woman's Rule 2: The War

-Life and Banishment of Apophis: book 1

-The Kidney Friendly Diet

-The Ultimate Hemp Cookbook

-Creating a Dispensary(legally)

-Cleanliness throughout life: the importance of showering from childhood to adulthood.

-Strong Roots: The Risks of Overcoddling children

-Hemp Horoscopes: Cosmic Insights and Earthly Healing

- Celestial Hemp Navigating the Zodiac: Through the Green Cosmos

-Astrological Hemp: Aligning The Stars with Earth's Ancient Herb

-The Astrological Guide to Hemp: Stars, Signs, and Sacred Leaves

-Green Growth: Innovative Marketing Strategies for your Hemp Products and Dispensary
-Cosmic Cannabis
-Astrological Munchies
-Henry The Hemp
-Zodiacal Roots: The Astrological Soul Of Hemp

Check out my Virtual dispensary for all your hemp needs: https://shift.store/sg1fan23477/retail

If you want solar for your home go here: https://www.harborsolar.live/apophisenterprises/
Instagrams: @apophis_enterprises, @hempkingdom2024, @apophisbookemporium, @apophisfashion, @apophisscardshop
Twitter: @apophisenterpr1, Tiktok:@apophisenterprise
Youtube: @sg1fan23477
Podcast: Apophis Chat Zone: https://open.spotify.com/show/5zXbrCLEV2xzCp8ybrfHsk?si=fb4d4fdbdce44dec
Newsletter: https://apophiss-newsletter-27c897.beehiiv.com/